Pickles and Preserves

Homeworld

The Publisher:
Lone Pine Publishing
#206, 10426-81 Avenue
Edmonton, Alberta, Canada
T6E 1X5

Canadian Cataloguing in Publication Data
    Pickles and preserves

    (Homeworld)
    ISBN 0-919433-88-X

    1. Pickles. 2. Canning and preserving. I. Series.
TX805.P53 1990   641.4'6   C90-091500-5

Editorial: Phillip R. Kennedy, Debra Rebryna, Doug Elves
Research: Keith Ashwell
Cover Design: Beata Kurpinski
Cover Photo: Yuet Chan
Printing: Friesen Printers. Altona, Manitoba, Canada

The publisher gratefully acknowledges the assistance of the Federal Department of Communications, Alberta Culture and Multiculturalism and the Alberta Foundation for the Arts in the production of this book

Contents

Acknowledgements

Special thanks are due to Ruth Kennedy for her advice and the following recipes: Corsican Olive Oil Pickles (p. 23), Grandma LaPointe's Harvest Pickles (p. 22), Dawne's Rosy Crabapples (p. 24), Cornichons de Noël (p. 37), Grandma Zastre's Mustard Pickles (p. 38), The Four C Pickle (p. 28) and Sweet and Sour Dills (p. 29), and to Thomas Anthony Kocourek for the French Pickle (p. 36) and Dill Pickle (p. 27) recipes and his many helpful comments.

Introduction

Modern food preservation began as a scientific curiosity in the eighteenth century, when biologists used bottled foods in their experiments. Although these first canners used sterilized, airtight jars, they did not process the bottled foods beforehand. Consequently, foods "preserved" by their methods spoiled quickly and were unsafe to eat.

During the French Revolution canning became safe and practical for the first time. Nicholas Appert, a chef and confectioner, discovered that canned foods which were boiled with a preserving agent stayed preserved for long periods of time. He relied on two simple but effective preservatives: sugar and vinegar. These had been found to stop the decaying action of enzymes, molds, yeasts and bacteria.

A few decades later, an American, Thomas Kensett, invented the tin can, which was easier to mass-produce than the older glass jars. Today, most commercially processed meats, fruits and vegetables are sold in descendants of Kensett's original cans.

In the latter part of this century more elaborate (and sometimes controversial) ways of preserving food were developed, such as blast-freezing, commercial dehydration and irradiation.

This book's not about high-tech methods of preserving foods, but about those used by our parents and grandparents to stock their kitchen cupboards. It contains safe, step-by-step directions for how to make delicious chutneys, pickles and relishes using simple equipment and everyday kitchen supplies.

Of course, it's much quicker to get pickles and relishes from the supermarket. It's much more satisfying, however, to open and enjoy a jar of pickles made with a personal recipe or to send a bottle of preserves as a special gift. Home canning also gives gardeners a realistic, economical way to save the products of their summer's work.

Try these recipes. Experiment with new herbs and combinations of spices. Use this book as a guide to the infinite, exciting flavours of the world just outside your door.

Before You Begin

The prospective canner should be prepared to preserve foods in quantity. It is more economical to make several jars of pickles, chutneys, relishes or salted vegetables than to make just one.

A Kitchen Checklist

Make sure you have reasonably large stainless-steel or glass bowls, or enamelled pans. These must be unchipped, as even the smallest chip can be an ideal place for bacteria to breed, however careful the pre-cleaning. Small nicks can also lead to further chipping, and consequent contamination of the food.

When boiling and then simmering, use pans that are large enough to handle a given quantity of ingredients and liquids. They should not be made of copper, brass or zinc, as these metals will react with vinegar, lemon juice and salt and taint the finished product.

Wooden or plastic ladles and stirring spoons will be needed. Your kitchen should also have on hand measuring bowls, for both liquids and solids, a measuring scale, and some well-sharpened paring knives. Cheesecloth is also required, since certain spices such as cloves, cinnamon sticks and bay leaves must be contained in a cheesecloth bag for processing.

Containers

Most brands of canning jars (Mason jars) are composed of three distinct parts: the glass jar itself, a screw-top ring and the flat metal lid. Wash the jars thoroughly and sterilize them with boiling water before using them, no matter how clean they look (see p. 44). It is not safe to assume that the jars will be sufficiently sterilized when they are immersed in a hot-water bath during processing. Additionally, any jar which is going to receive hot preserves should be warmed beforehand to prevent shattering.

Old screw-top rings may be used over and over again, provided that they are in good condition and hold the lid securely in place. Never re-use old lids, however. The sealing compound along their rims is only effective once; they will not safely seal again. Always buy a new set of lids for each new batch of preserves.

Some older jars (Bell jars) with glass lids may still be in circulation. If this type of container is to be used, be sure to replace the disposable rubber ring which makes a seal between the lid and the jar.

Cheesecloth Bag

Canning Jars

Jam jars and preserving jars come in a number of sizes. The more popular sizes begin at 360 mL (12 oz. or one half-pint). These small jam jars are sometimes distinctively decorated on the outer surface. Canning jars are commonly available in the following range of sizes:

Imperial	Metric
1/2 pint	285 mL
1 pint	570 mL
1 quart	1,130 mL
2 quarts	2,260 mL

Any recipe that involves fermentation in the jar, sterilizing in hot water baths or putting very hot mixtures into jars should not employ "re-cycled" store jars. For such recipes use commercial home canning containers that are made from appropriately tempered glass and have seal caps and screw tops that will ensure an impenetrable seal. Other cold-process preserves can be stored in commercial jam and pickle jars.

Go through a checklist of all possible kitchen requirements before going to a supermarket or farmer's market to buy your fruits or vegetables in quantity or in bulk. The essence of good results is the freshness of the produce in the first place. Valuable time can be lost if you suddenly have to chase down a stray cheesecloth or a hidden thermometer.

The Essential Ingredients

Obviously, at the top of the list are those fruits and vegetables you intend to preserve.

But there are other essentials, namely vinegar, salt, sugar and spices. If you want your recipe to deliver on its promise, the vinegar, salt and sugar should be the right kind for the recipe and the spices as fresh as possible. Even the water has to be exactly "right."

Fruits

Whether hand-picked or bulk-bought they first need a close examination for bruising, molds, over-ripeness and contamination with soil. Remove suspicious fruits and wash the rest thoroughly but gently.

To prevent discolouration in fruits that have to be peeled, cored and sliced or diced you can store them temporarily in a brine solution (5 mL of salt to 1 litre of water) or in an ascorbic acid (vitamin C) solution (0.5 mL of powder to one litre of water). Reconstituted lemon juice may be used instead of ascorbic acid powder (0.5 mL of lemon juice to one litre of water); fresh lemon juice should not be used, as the acidity of fresh lemons is quite unpredictable.

Vegetables

Go through the same rejection process as for fruits, looking particularly for discolouration or extreme softness. Soil, which contains potentially harmful bacteria and mold spores, should be gently scrubbed off.

The canner is responsible for choosing the youngest and freshest produce available. Substandard or flavourless vegetables will result in inferior preserves.

Pickling cucumbers are more difficult to select. They should be nearly mature and solid to the touch. Try to select cucumbers that are between 6 and 8 cm long, as this is a convenient size for pickling. When you're washing pickling cucumbers, remove those that float to the surface— they will probably make hollow pickles. They are almost certainly improperly developed, but they needn't go to waste, as they can be diced for relishes and chutneys.

Salt

Salt, or sodium chloride, is a safe and effective preservative. It stops the action of most enzymes and inhibits the growth of bacteria. Most supermarkets sell special pickling salts, which contain pure sodium chloride. Everyday table salt is not suitable for canning, as it contains certain chemicals which allow easy, lump-free pouring; these will form an undesirable sediment. Household salt also contains iodine, which darkens and discolours preserved foods.

Spices

Packs of pickling spices are readily available in stores. The best pickles use spices in their whole form (seeds or leaves). Allspice, bay leaves, cardamom, cayenne and chili peppers, cinnamon sticks, coriander seed, whole cloves, dill seed, dried ginger shavings, mace, mustard seed, whole nutmeg and green and black peppercorns can all be used for pickling. Garlic is also a valuable spice for the canner; however, because it carries some natural bacteria, garlic should first be scalded briefly.

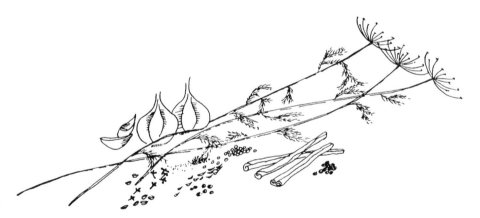

Selected Recipes

Chutneys

In India chutneys are served as a traditional condiment with everyday meals. Today chutneys are enjoyed worldwide, a delicacy to many people because of their delightful blend of sweet and sour flavours. As a rule, chutneys are coarser than relishes and have larger chunks of fruits and vegetables.

Apple Chutney

2.25 kg tart cooking apples
l kg sugar
680 g chopped raisins
2 L malt vinegar
30 g crushed garlic
120 g salt
60 g mustard seeds
60 g ground ginger
10 g cayenne

Wash, core and slice the apples, but do not peel them. Boil these ingredients until thoroughly soft, then add the spices. Pour the boiling mixture into bottles and seal securely.

Allow the chutney to mature for at least two months before serving.

Apricot Chutney

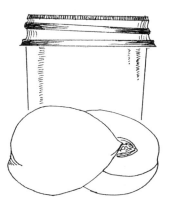

2 kg apricots
1 medium lemon
250 mL sugar
250 mL brown sugar
60 mL cider vinegar
15 mL ground ginger
5 mL allspice
5 mL dry mustard
Dash of nutmeg
120 mL chopped onion
240 mL raisins

Wash and quarter the apricots after discarding the stones. Peel and chop the lemon. Combine other ingredients in a large pan and bring to a boil. Add apricots to the spice and fruit mixture and bring to boil. Simmer 45 minutes, stirring frequently.

Fill canning jars with chutney to 0.5 cm of top. Run a spatula around the inside edge of the jar to remove air bubbles. Seal and place the jars on a canning kettle rack almost full of hot water. Fill the kettle to cover the jars by at least 5 cm and simmer for 5 minutes. When cool, store jars in a dark cupboard for at least two months.

Green Tomato Chutney

3 kg green tomatoes
500 g silverskin onions
1 kg cooking apples
1 red beet
one quarter head cauliflower
250 g carrots
750 mL malt vinegar
450 g brown sugar
450 g molasses

Blanch, peel tomatoes and quarter. Peel onions. Peel, core and quarter apples. Peel beet and make into small cubes. Reduce cauliflower to florets only. Dice scraped carrots finely. Liquify vinegar, sugar and molasses in large pot, over heat. Add vegetables and bring to boil.

15 ml salt
15 mL freshly ground black pepper
5 mL mace
5 mL cayenne pepper
5 mL freshly ground nutmeg
30 mL Worchestershire sauce
340 g raisins

Add these to mixture.

3 peeled garlic cloves
6 whole cloves
3 bay leaves

Tie these in cheesecloth and suspend in chutney. Reduce heat to a simmer. Stir frequently for about 2 hours or until mixture thickens. Pour into sterilized jars. Leave 1 cm (1/2 in) headspace and process in hot water for 10 minutes. Allow to cool. Check that the lids are very tight. Store for two to three months to let the flavours mingle and mature.

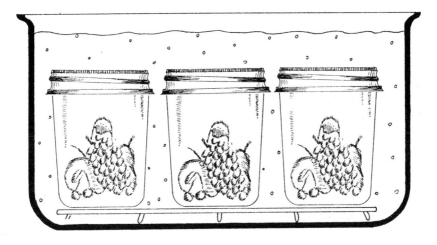

A Canning Kettle or Canner

Peach & Mango
Chutney

4 large ripe mangoes
1 kg peaches
1 large onion, sliced
1 green pepper, seeded and diced
1 peeled garlic clove, mashed
10 mL cinnamon
2.5 mL ground cloves
2.5 mL allspice
pinch of cayenne pepper
5 mL salt
350 g raisins
350 g white sugar
500 mL white vinegar

Peel mangoes, discard seeds and slice. Blanch peaches, remove stones and slice. Bring the spices, sugar and vinegar to a boil and simmer for 1 hour or until quite syrupy. Add mangoes and peaches and continue simmering until fruit is tender.

Pour into sterilized jars. Leave 1 cm headspace and process in a hot-water bath. Head space should be 1 cm.

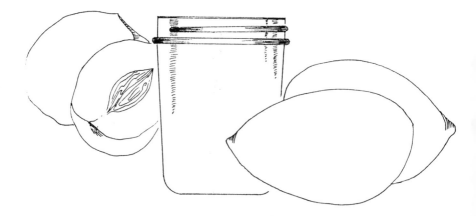

Pickles

Pickled Baby Corn

(Makes 2.3 kg)

2 kg baby corn
250 mL water
500 mL sugar
500 mL vinegar
10 mL salt
15 mL pickling spice

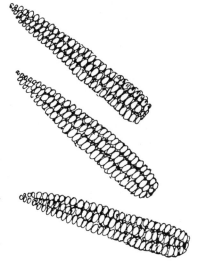

Husk and clean corn and boil for 5 minutes. Drain and set aside. Tie pickling spices in cheesecloth with a draw string. Boil water, vinegar and spices for 5 minutes. Pack drained corn ears in sterilized jars; cover with spiced vinegar. Seal and process for 10 minutes in boiling water.

Pickled Beets

(Makes 1 L)

2 dozen small red beets
120 mL cider vinegar
120 g white sugar
120 g brown sugar
10 mL pickling spices

Boil beets until tender, then briefly immerse in cold water and skin them. Boil vinegar, sugar and spices vigorously for 5 minutes, then strain out spices. Pack beets into sterilized jars, pour pickling liquid to cover, leave 1 cm headspace and process in boiling water for 30 minutes.

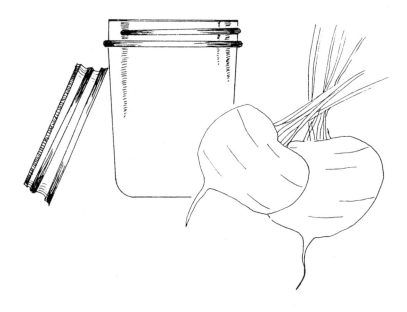

Pickled Carrots

(Makes 2 L)

2.5 kg carrots, young and crisp
500 mL boiling water

Peel carrots. Cut into sticks. Boil 5 minutes and drain.

750 mL pickling salt
750 mL white vinegar
500 mL water
500 mL white sugar
15 mL pickling spice

Mix the liquid and powdered ingredients. Put the pickling spice in a cheesecloth bag, and immerse in the mixture. Bring to a vigorous boil, remove spice bag and cook carrots until tender. Strain carrots, saving the liquid. Pack into preserving jars, and cover with pickling liquid. Seal and store.

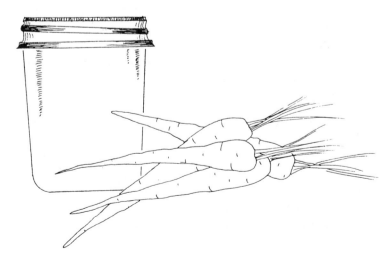

Grandma LaPointe's
Harvest Pickles

850 g small pickling cucumbers
850 g green tomatoes, cored and coarsely chopped
850 g sweet onions, peeled and sliced
2 sweet yellow peppers, cut into thin strips
2 sweet red peppers, cut into thin strips
255 mL salt
4 L ice water
240 mL yellow beans, cut into 3 cm lengths
480 mL lima beans
400 g baby carrots
480 mL celery, cut into 3 cm pieces
1 medium cauliflower, cut into small pieces
2 L vinegar
1.8 L sugar
80 mL pickling spices
60 mL mustard seed
30 mL celery seed

Wash vegetables, cut cucumbers in half and slice very thinly. Combine cucumbers, tomatoes, onions, peppers in a large bowl. Dissolve 240 mL salt into the ice water and pour over the vegetables. Cover and let stand for 18 hours at room temperature. Drain, pour boiling water over vegetables, and drain immediately. Set aside.

Put the carrots, celery, cauliflower and all of the beans into a large pot. Add 15 mL salt and enough water to cover the mixture. Cover and cook for approximately 20 minutes, then drain. Combine with the cucumber mix.

Put the mustard seed, celery seed and pickling spices into a cheesecloth bag. Add vinegar, sugar and the spice bag to the pot of vegetables. Slowly bring to a boil and simmer for about 10 minutes. Remove the spice bag.

Fill hot sterilized jars with the mixture, leaving 0.5 cm headspace. Wipe jars and rims with clean, damp cloth, and place tops on jars. Process in a boiling water bath for 5 minutes.

Corsican Olive Oil Pickles

24 small pickling cucumbers
240 mL salt
960 mL vinegar
120 mL olive oil (Spanish olive oil gives a nuttier flavour)
60 mL sugar
60 mL mustard seed
60 mL celery seed

Wash cucumbers, peel and cut crosswise in thin slices. Layer the slices and soak in a brine solution in a large crock or glass bowl. Cover and let stand 12-18 hours at room temperature. Drain. Rinse well with cold water.

Combine vinegar, olive oil, sugar and spices; boil 1 minute. Add cucumbers; simmer until cucumbers change colour. Pack cucumbers into pint jars and pour hot syrup over the cucumbers, leaving 0.5 cm headspace. Process in boiling water bath for 5 minutes. Remove jars and complete seals.

Dawne's Rosy Crabapples

2 kg rosy crabapples with stems
1 L 5% cider vinegar
1 L water
1.6 L sugar
38 mL whole cloves
38 mL whole allspice
4 sticks whole cinnamon

Wash crabapples in cold water. Remove blossoms but leave the stems on. Prick crabapples with a wooden skewer. Bring the vinegar, water, sugar and spices to a boil. Add the crabapples to the spice and syrup mixture and cook for 6-8 minutes. Remove crabapples with a slotted spoon and pack in sterilized jars. Pour the syrup over the crabapples, leaving 0.5 cm of headspace. Seal and process in a boiling water bath for 10 minutes.

Pickled Red Cabbage

(Makes 1 L)

1 medium red cabbage head
1 cooking apple (Granny Smith)
100 mL dry red wine
5 mL salt
15 mL butter

Shred cabbage. Peel, core and dice apple. Place in pan, add wine, salt and butter and simmer until cabbage is just limp.

250 mL dry red wine
60 mL red wine vinegar
60 mL brown sugar
2 cloves

Add wine, wine vinegar, sugar and cloves to cabbage, then simmer for 90 minutes. Before proceeding to serve or process, remove the cloves. Sealing and sterilizing in a hot water bath takes 30 minutes.

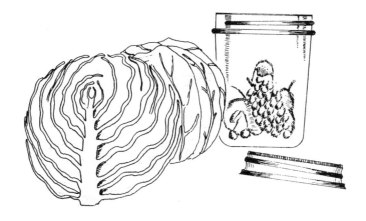

Zucchini Pickles

(Makes 2.5 L)

2.5 L zucchini
500 mL onions
2 L water
125 mL pickling salt

Thinly slice zucchini and onions. Bring water and salt to a boil. Turn off heat and soak vegetables in brine for 3 hours. Drain and rinse zucchini well

500 mL white vinegar
250 mL white sugar
5 mL celery seed
5 mL mustard seed
5 mL turmeric
2 mL dry mustard

Bring vinegar, sugar and spices to a boil and simmer for 10 minutes. Pack zucchini and onions in sterilized jars. Cover with liquid leaving 1.5 cm headspace. Seal and boil for 5 minutes.

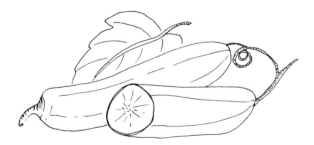

Dill Pickles

12 pickling cucumbers
1.4 L cold water
200 mL vinegar
120 mL salt
handful of fresh dill

Remove any cucumber blossoms. Scrub vegetables gently but firmly under cold running water and wipe dry. Put the dill and the cucumbers into the jars. Make a brine solution with the water, vinegar and salt, and pour over cucumbers, leaving 1.5 cm of headspace. It is important that the cucumbers remain totally submerged in the brine. The pickles should be stored in a cool, dry place, and should be ready to eat in six to eight weeks.

Troubleshooter's Hints

Pickles are soft:
- cucumber blossoms, which carry softening enzymes, were not removed during cleaning.

Pickles are pale or bleached:
- the contents of the jar were exposed to light. Keep the next batch in a darker place.

Pickles are hollow:
- the pickling cucumbers were substandard (see p. 10)
- the cucumbers were stale.

The Four C Pickle

1 L celery, cut into 5 cm strips
500 mL carrots, peeled and cut into 2 cm strips
500 mL small cauliflower flowerets
1 kg small pickling cucumbers, sliced
1 kg small onions
500 mL of any kind of sweet pepper, chopped
60 mL Dijon mustard
1 L cider vinegar
120 mL salt
900 mL sugar
300 mL mustard seed
45 mL celery seed
4 mL whole cloves
3 mL ground turmeric

Prepare onions by peeling and quartering. Prepare the remaining vegetables as specified above.

Combine the Dijon mustard and vinegar in a large pot. Blend well, and add salt, sugar, mustard seed, celery seed, and the remainder of the spices. Bring to a slow boil. Add the vegetables, then slowly bring the mixture back to a boil.

Fill hot sterilized jars with vegetable mixture and syrup, leaving 0.5 cm of headroom. Wipe jar and rim with a clean damp cloth. Process in a boiling water bath for 5 minutes. Remove jars and complete seals.

Sweet and Sour Dills

2 kg small pickling cucumbers
2 large, sweet yellow onions, peeled and sliced thinly
120 mL dill seeds or 16 heads of fresh dill
1.4 L cider vinegar
1.4 L sugar
90 mL salt
10 mL mustard seed
10 mL celery seed

Wash cucumbers and cut them crosswise in 0.5 cm slices. Place 2 slices of sweet yellow onion and 1 dill head into each hot sterilized jar.

Combine vinegar, sugar, salt, mustard seed and celery seed in a large pot. Bring to a boil. While the syrup is boiling, pack cucumbers into the jars and pour the syrup over the cucumbers, leaving 0.5 cm of headroom. Wipe rims with clean, damp cloth and adjust lids.

Process pint jars for 10 minutes in a boiling water bath. Remove jars and complete seals.

Troubleshooting

Pickles are tough:
- too much salt was used.
- too much vinegar was used

Pickles are dark:
- table salt was used instead of pickling salt.
- pickles were exposed to air.

Brine is cloudy:
- pickles were stored in a warm place.
- table salt was used.

Relishes

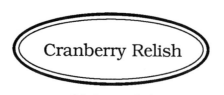

Cranberry Relish

(Makes 2.5 L)

1 L cranberries, fresh or frozen
1 medium orange
1 cup raisins
1 medium onion, chopped
1 green pepper, seeded,
    chopped
1 garlic clove, mashed
30 mL freshly grated ginger
250 mL cider vinegar
1 can frozen cranberry juice

Wash and coarsely chop cranberries and place them in a pan. Remove outer peel of the orange and set aside. Remove pith from orange and separate the sections. Coarsely chop the peel and orange sections in a blender or food processor and add to the cranberries. Add onions, green pepper and garlic to the cranberry mixture. Stir in the ginger vinegar and cranberry juice.

Bring to a boil and simmer for 10 minutes, stirring frequently to prevent burning.

480 mL white sugar
2 mL salt
1 mL cayenne
1 mL ground cloves
5 mL mustard seed

Add the above to a pot and continue simmering for 30 minutes or until desired thickness is achieved. Fill half-quart jars, allowing 1.5 cm headspace. Process for 10 minutes.

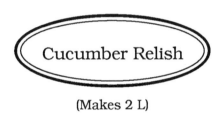

Cucumber Relish

(Makes 2 L)

12 large cucumbers
4 green peppers
4 large onions
120 mL pickling salt

Skin cucumbers, remove seeds and slice. Remove seeds from the green peppers and finely chop. Finely chop onions. Mix thoroughly with salt and let stand overnight in a glass bowl or crock pot.

240 mL white sugar
5 mL celery seed
15 mL mustard seed
240 mL horseradish

Transfer the vegetables to a cooking pot, add the remaining ingredients and bring to boil and simmer for 15 minutes. Seal and process for 5 minutes.

Ripe Tomato Relish

(Makes 2 L)

3 kg ripe tomatoes
7 medium onions
240 mL pure salt

Scald, peel and chop tomatoes. Chop onions finely, add salt and let stand overnight. Before proceeding, strain excess moisture through cheesecloth.

240 mL chopped celery
2 diced green peppers
480 mL sugar
480 mL cider vinegar
2.5 mL cinnamon
2.5 mL mustard seed

Mix all ingredients. Bring briefly to a boil and let cool completely. This relish can be immediately sealed and chilled for general use. It will keep refrigerated for about one year.

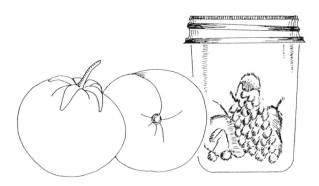

Tomato & Apple Relish

(Makes 2 L)

2 kg ripe tomatoes
about 4 cooking apples (Granny Smith)
950 mL onions
2 red peppers
2 green peppers

Blanch, peel and chop tomatoes. Peel, core and chop apples. Chop onions, remove pepper seeds and chop peppers finely.

240 mL raisins
100 mL brown sugar
240 mL cider vinegar
15 mL mustard seed
10 mL celery seed
5 mL salt
5 mL turmeric

Combine raisins, sugar vinegar and seasonings. Bring to a brief boil and then add tomatoes, apples, onions and peppers. Bring all the ingredients briefly to a boil and then simmer for 1 hour or until relish is thickened, stirring frequently. Fill sterilized jars to within 1.5 cm headspace and process in boiling water for 15 minutes.

Summer Relish

(Makes 2 L)

3 kg ripe tomatoes
360 mL peaches
2 large cooking apples
2 large pears
4 onions
2 sweet red peppers
125 g green seedless grapes

Blanch tomatoes and peaches. Peel and dice. Peel, core and dice apples and pears. Chop onions, remove pepper seeds and chop. Quarter grapes. Mix all above ingredients together.

750 mL cider vinegar
340 g sugar
30 mL salt
75 mL pickling spice

Tie spices in cheesecloth. Heat vinegar to dissolve sugar and salt. Combine all ingredients, bring to a boil and then simmer for 1 hour or until desired thickness is reached. Remove spices. Pour into sterilized containers and let cool before sealing tightly. Will keep refrigerated for up to one year.

Hot Chili Sauce

(Makes 1 L)

2 kg ripe tomatoes
1 large onion
200 mL sugar
350 mL cider vinegar
5 mL seedless red peppers
5 mL mustard seed
5 mL salt
2.5 mL ground ginger
2.5 mL fresh nutmeg
2.5 mL curry powder

Blanch tomatoes and chop onions into small rough pieces. Combine all ingredients in a large pot, bring to a boil, then simmer for two hours or until desired thickness is obtained, stirring frequently. Fill jars to 1 cm of top. Process in boiling water bath for 15 minutes. Check that the seal is tight. This is an excellent relish for hamburgers and hot dogs.

French Pickle

1.4 L green tomatoes
500 mL onions
500 mL vinegar
120 mL salt
2 large cucumbers
1 bunch celery
6 sweet red peppers

Chop vegetables finely, then sprinkle them with salt. Let the mixture stand overnight, and drain the juice off. Cook in vinegar for 15 minutes, then blend in the sauce and seal while still hot.

French Pickle Sauce

1.4 kg white sugar
240 mL flour
5 mL mustard seed
5 mL celery seed
5 mL curry powder
5 mL ground mustard
5 mL turmeric

Mix ingredients together and cook over low heat for about half an hour, stirring slowly. When the sauce begins to boil, continue to cook it for five to ten minutes.

Cornichons de Noël

10 large cucumbers
2 large green peppers, seeded and cut into strips
2 large sweet yellow peppers, seeded and cut into strips
2 large sweet red peppers, seeded and cut into strips
2 medium sweet yellow onions
1.2 L sugar
960 mL vinegar
850 mL diced celery
240 mL water
120 mL salt
10 mL mustard seed

Peel cucumbers and dice into cubes, leaving the seeds in. Place in a large bowl and sprinkle with salt. Cover and let stand in a cool dry place for at least 18 hours. Drain and rinse well.

Put peppers, celery, onions, sugar, vinegar, mustard seed, celery seed and water into a large pot. Add the diced cucumbers. Slowly bring to a boil, stirring occasionally. When the cucumbers become translucent the mixture is done.

Fill hot sterilized jars with the mixture, leaving 0.5 cm of headspace. Process in a hot water bath for 15 minutes.

Grandma Zastre's
Mustard Pickles

650 g pickling cucumbers
480 mL chopped onion
2 large green peppers, seeded and chopped
1 medium head cauliflower, cut into small pieces
480 mL pearl onions, peeled
960 mL sugar
960 mL cider vinegar
240 mL salt
180 mL flour
60 mL dry mustard
15 mL celery salt
8 mL ground turmeric

Wash vegetables and chop cucumbers. Layer cucumbers, onion, peppers, cauliflower, pearl onions and salt in a large bowl. Cover with cold water and let stand for 18 hours in a cool dry place. Drain and rinse well.

Combine sugar, vinegar, flour and the remainder of the spices in a large pot. Blend well, and slowly bring to a boil, stirring constantly to avoid burning the mixture. Add the vegetables, bring back to a boil and simmer for about 12 minutes.

Fill hot sterilized jars with the mixture, leaving 0.5 cm headspace. Process in a boiling water bath for 15 minutes. Remove jars.

Salting Vegetables

This is one of the oldest methods of preserving food known to man. Salting protects foods against spoilage by dehydrating them; additionally, many microorganisms cannot live in very salty environments. Almost any food, from meat to fish to vegetables can be preserved in this way. This chapter, however, is concerned with vegetables that are popular choices for salting.

Salted Beans

Both French Beans and the Scarlet Runner variety are recommended.

Cut the ends off fresh, young beans. String them if necessary and slice runner beans diagonally. To preserve, simply pack beans into a suitable jar, alternating layers of beans with layers of salt. As a rule of thumb, you should use 1 kg of pickling salt to 3 kg of beans. Cover loosely and store in a cool, dark spot for 4 or 5 days. By then the contents should have shrunk. Refill as before.

At this time the jars should be tightly sealed. The beans will stay fresh for 6 months. To serve, first drain the beans in cold, running water. Then soak them in lukewarm water for a maximum of 2 hours. Cook until tender.

Sauerkraut

Sauerkraut is salted cabbage that is allowed to ferment. It has been a staple of well-stocked farm larders for centuries.

Buy or pick your own cabbages while they are still firm. Remove outer leaves and cut away any bruising and wash.

Quarter the cabbage and cut out the solid stem. Now shred the cabbage as finely as possible. Some specialty stores sell a cabbage shredder which may also be used.

Weigh the cabbage. For every 2 kg of cabbage you will require 45 mL of pickling salt.

Mix cabbage and salt thoroughly. Press firmly down into a large, open-mouthed crock, filling it to the brim. Cover the surface with a piece of clean cheesecloth, and then set a plate on top of it; if necessary, weigh the plate down with a heavy stone or concrete block. The plate should keep the cabbage immersed in the brine. If a film forms during the next 10 days skim it off and replace the cheesecloth.

Once the liquid level drops significantly fermentation is almost complete. Re-top the crock with a brine made of 30 mL pickling salt to 950 mL of water.

Sauerkraut can be eaten without further processing after six to eight weeks.

For long-term storage, drain the brine from the cabbage, bring to a boil and add the cabbage and then let simmer for a few minutes. The sauerkraut should then be processed in sterilized jars for 30 minutes. Before storage make sure the seals are absolutely tight.

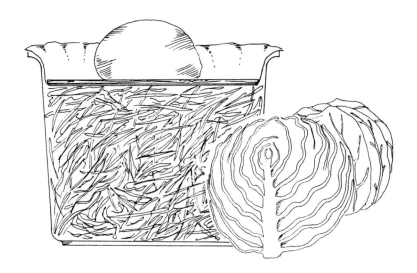

Sauerkraut Crock

Troubleshooting

Sauerkraut is pinkish:
• the crock was too hot during fermentation. Keep the next batch in a cooler place.
• not enough salt was used.

Sauerkraut is dark:
• the contents of the crock were contaminated with iron. Iron utensils and containers should not be used to prepare sauerkraut.
• the contents of the crock were exposed to air. Always ensure that the cabbage is below the level of the brine.

Sauerkraut is soft:
• not enough salt was used, or the salt was not distributed evenly.
• the cabbage may have been exposed to air.

Any sauerkraut that seems bad should be discarded immediately.

Glossary

Blanching

Blanching is a must for preserving some fruits and vegetables, as the process not only stops the ripening action of a plant's enzymes but also kills almost all potentially dangerous bacteria.

The food to be blanched is first placed in a wire basket, colander or wire skimmer, and is then lowered into a pot of boiling water for twenty to thirty seconds. The food is then quickly immersed in cold water to stop the cooking process.

Peaches, tomatoes and silverskin onions are peeled much more easily if they have been blanched beforehand.

Brine

Quite simply, a brine is a solution of salt and water. Some recipes recommend a brief brine treatment to prevent fruits from being discoloured, others use the brine for its preservative qualities or for the distinct flavour it gives to vegetables. Brines keep vegetables crisp, since the salt draws moisture from the vegetables.

Brine strengths should not be tampered with, as they have specific purposes. For example, weak brines are used to prepare vegetables for pickles and relishes; stronger brines are used to preserve vegetables for long periods of time. Only pickling salt should be used for making brines. (see p. 10)

Fermentation

Fermentation is the name for any chemical process that breaks down natural sugars into various other substances. One kind of fermentation, used in making beer and wine, creates alcohol. Another kind produces lactic acid, a strong preservative agent; vegetables like cabbage, rutabagas and turnips are preserved by this method.

The process begins with a mixture of pickling salt and vegetables. The salt speeds up the vegetables' natural fermentation while stopping any spoilage or decay. Vegetables preserved in this way must be boiled before eating.

Headspace

Headspace is the amount of space between the top of the jar and its contents. If the jar doesn't have enough headspace, it could explode when the contents of the jar try to expand. If the jar has too much, its contents may become discoloured; but worse, an airtight seal may not form, giving harmful bacteria room to breed.

Spoilage

Spoilage is a natural stage in the growth of fruits and vegetables. Most spoilage is caused by the action of enzymes, molds or bacteria on food; efficient canning slows or stops these agents of decomposition.

Enzymes change the chemical composition of foods. They make tomatoes redden and peaches ripen; they also cause fruits and vegetables to decompose and lose their texture, taste and colour. Heat, sugar, salt and vinegar all stop enzymes in their tracks.

Microorganisms also spoil food. Many harmful microorganisms can be removed by simply washing fruits and vegetables. Yeasts and molds are slowed down considerably at 0°C; sterilization in boiling water is the only sure way to kill bacteria and molds, as some produce spores which resist freezing temperatures.

Bacteria are the most difficult microorganisms to destroy, and are also the most deadly.

One bacterium, *Staphylococcus aureus*, is the most common cause of food poisoning in Canada. Personal cleanliness, careful washing of foodstuffs and cooking utensils, and strict adherence to recipe instructions will greatly reduce the risk of staphylococcus contamination.

Clostridium botulinum, also known as botulism, is a fearful killer. It exists in common soil in a completely harmless, spore form. It produces a lethal toxin when it reproduces in food. Fortunately, adequate heat and sanitary food preparation make botulism outbreaks relatively rare.

Sterilization

All parts of a canning jar must be sterilized shortly before use. The glass pieces should first be washed with hot water and dishwashing detergent, and then rinsed. The jars should then be turned upside-down and boiled in water which rises at least five cemtimetres above the jar tops. Fifteen minutes of boiling is required for complete sterilization. Leave the jars in hot water until you're ready to use them. A dishwasher can be used, if set at the highest temperature.

An oven may also be used for sterilization. In this method, the jars should be washed and rinsed as above, and then heated in an oven at 100°C for fifteen minutes.

Some metal lids may require different sterilization methods than those described above. It is best to refer to the manufacturer's instructions when sterilizing lids.

Sugar and Honey

Buy white or brown sugar or molasses, as indicated in the recipe. For a richer taste, half of the required sugar may be replaced with honey, but honeys that have a distinct flavour should be avoided, as they might produce an unwanted aftertaste.

Vinegar

Home-made vinegar is not recommended, as the sediment which forms from it may interfere with preserving. Therefore, you should buy distilled vinegars, whether cider, malt, wine or white. Look for those that have a strength rating on the label of 6% acetic acid. Vinegars of 7% or stronger are not appropriate for these recipes.

A pickling vinegar is simply vinegar flavoured with herbs and spices. A standard mix for use in pickling vinegars can be found in any major supermarket. Some recipes may recommend certain combinations of spices, but there's always room to experiment.

A quick pickling vinegar can be made by boiling the spices and vinegar for three to five minutes. Wise cooks, however, will prepare a bag of spices and leave it in a large jug of vinegar for a few weeks.

If the resulting combination of flavours is too spicy, do not dilute the vinegar. Rather, adjust the taste with sugar, brown sugar or molasses. For making sour pickles you should add 100 g of sugar to 1 L of vinegar. Double the amount of sugar for medium pickles, and for sweet pickles double the amount again.

Water

Tap water is probably hard and contains purifying minerals and filtering agents. This can lead to darkened fruits and vegetables and a softening of the ingredients.

It's easy to provide softwater for your preserve projects. Boil about 4 litres of water with one teaspoonful of baking soda for fifteen minutes and let it stand overnight. The next day, remove the film (if any) that has formed on the water's surface (when pouring or ladling, you should be careful not to disturb or stir up the mineral sediment at the bottom).

Conversion Tables

Volume

1 L	= 0.264 gal.
	= 1.76 pt.
	= 2.11 qt.
	= 4.54 cups

1 gal.	= 3.785 L
1 pt.	= 473 mL
1 qt.	= 946 mL
1 cup	= 240 mL
1 Tsp	= 15 mL
1 tsp	= 5 mL

Weight

1 g	= 0.0353 oz.
1 kg	= 2.296 lbs.

1 oz.	= 28.35 g
1 lb.	= 435.6 g

Length

1 cm = 0.3937 in.   1 inch = 2.54 cm

Temperature

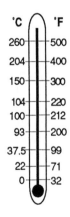

°C	°F
260	500
204	400
150	300
104	220
100	212
93	200
37.5	99
22	71
0	32

Index to Recipes